got creativity?

Your notebook for success through
creativity and courage.

MICHAEL BALCH

GOT CREATIVITY?
YOUR NOTEBOOK FOR SUCCESS THROUGH CREATIVITY AND COURAGE.

iUniverse books may be ordered through booksellers or by contacting:

iUniverse
1663 Liberty Drive
Bloomington, IN 47403
www.iuniverse.com
1-800-Authors (1-800-288-4677)

ISBN: 978-1-4917-7231-7 (sc)
ISBN: 978-1-4917-7462-5 (hc)
ISBN: 978-1-4917-7232-4 (e)

Print information available on the last page.

iUniverse rev. date: 8/17/2015

Contents

"Where all think alike, no one thinks very much."

Walter Lippmann, writer

Introduction

I believe that the cornerstone to successfully marketing or selling a product, or an idea, is CREATIVITY. We live in a world of the status quo. For those who continue to follow those in front of us, we will rarely get ahead. There may be nothing wrong with safety in numbers or following the herd. After all, if the herd, or group, succeeds then you will also. However, if they fail, you do too. Believe it or not there is comfort in knowing that others also failed. I struggle with the concept "one fail, all fail." I believe if I am going to fail, it is on me. I also believe that if I am going to succeed, it is mostly because of me. I believe in controlling my own destiny. I know that sounds enticing, but you need courage to successfully do it. If you have ambitions to be very successful, you need to get out of your rut and find your own path. To be uber successful in today's competitive environment you need to be "extraordinary or out-of-the-ordinary." Inside the herd, there is one, or a few people, that are better than everyone else. Those are the people that everyone else is chasing. It is a big game of "follow the leader." Those leaders being chased are the "extraordinary." This is the work environment that most people find themselves in. This "notebook" focuses on the people I refer to as "out-of-the-ordinary". These are the people that get off the beaten path and differentiate themselves. These are the Bill Gates, Richard

Branson, and Steve Jobs of this world. There is no reason why you can't be like them. The only thing you need is CREATIVITY and COURAGE. We are all born with CREATIVITY, however it is an ability that we have forgotten. This book is designed to bring out your inner CREATIVITY. Once you get your CREATIVE juices flowing, it is having the COURAGE to act on that CREATIVITY.

I refer to the book as a "notebook." This "notebook" is designed to be your idea book. The goal is for me to entice ideas out of you. You will notice plenty of blank pages for you to write down your thoughts and ideas. There is plenty of room for you to do exercises and put your thoughts on paper. This "notebook" is a living, breathing book of your ideas. Once you complete the "notebook," you should pick it up regularly to read your notes and to improve and act on them. I will motivate and inspire you to find your CREATIVITY and COURAGE. This will be a great start, but is up to you to complete it. Enjoy getting off the beaten path.

"Creativity requires the courage to let go of certainties."

Erich Fromm, psychologist and author

CHAPTER 1

What ever happened to CREATIVITY?

"Routine kills creative thought."

Scarlett Thomas, Author

Routines are the evil of progress. We have become creatures of habit. We live in a world of routines. There is safety in the idea of waking up each day and going through the same routine morning, noon and night. If we do that, our odds of safely going through the day with no surprises are high. The problem with that is that the odds of anything new and exciting happening are very low. When we choose hoe-hum over exciting we have low risk, but also low reward. Some would say society is in a rut and most people would agree, "being in a rut is not good." However, we have chosen to stay on the rails and continue life in the rut. It doesn't matter if we are talking about business or personal life, most people seem to follow the same path. We often think about getting out of the rut we are in, but most rarely act on it. Why don't we act on making a change? Is it fear? If we are willing to take the leap of faith, do we know how? What if we're wrong? Author, Speaker and Advisor on Education, Sir Kenneth Robinson noted "If you're not prepared to be wrong, you'll never come up with anything original." We, as a society are afraid of being wrong. It is safer to stay the course and live in the rut.

But is hoe-hum what you want? If it is, then there is no reason to read on. If you want more, read on. What would be the reason why we should get off the rails, take a different path, get out of the rut? Hopefully you have looked around at people that you view as successful and said, "I would like to be more like that person." You may have asked yourself, why are they successful? If we were to look at most successful people, the chances are that at some point they got off the beaten path. They moved in a different direction from the others. Deep within themselves, they found CREATIVITY and COURAGE. So often we look back at those

3

people and say "I wish I thought of that," or "I thought of doing that." The reality is whether you wish you had thought of that idea or someone acted on an idea you had, they had the CREATIVITY and COURAGE to make the change. They had the COURAGE to take a chance!!

CREATIVITY is something we are all born with, but may have lost. Fear not, it is not lost forever! CREATIVITY is a muscle inside of you that just needs a little exercise. It is deep inside the right side of your brain and wants to come out. The biggest obstacle to releasing that CREATIVITY is COURAGE. Psychologist and Author Erich Fromm says "creativity requires the courage to let go of certainties." CREATIVITY comes out in many forms. Sometimes we do some brainstorming to create a new idea, sometimes creative ideas happen by accident. Sometimes they happen because we make a similar decision to one we made in the past and got a different result. The question is, do you recognize the CREATIVE idea and have the COURAGE to act on the opportunity?

Here are a couple of examples of how I accidently created an opportunity. Approximately two years ago, I began commuting into the City of Chicago from my suburban home with my wife. I know what you are thinking…commuting with your wife takes COURAGE. If you know my wife, you would certainly agree. Just kidding; she's a great wife and mother. It's what happened as a result of that decision that bought me a commodity that we can never seem to get enough of. That commodity is TIME! Nobody can ever have enough time. Unfortunately, it is a finite commodity. My wife is a financial advisor at Merrill Lynch in downtown Chicago and, as I mentioned, we live in a suburb about half an hour outside the city. For over twenty years, she commuted by train to the city. She was sure that was the best way to go. She would tell people how reliable the train was. It was simple, half an hour in and half an hour back. No fuss, no muss. She was so comfortable with her commute. Ninety-nine percent of the time, it ran like clockwork. She sat in the same car, sat in the same seat, spoke with the same people. She was in a comfortable routine. She had no interest in change. The safety in her routine was comforting. She was no different than the millions of commuters that do the same thing every day, every week in every city in the world. Was she in a routine? Was she so comfortable and safe within that routine or did she lack COURAGE to explore ideas outside the routine? In order to save my marriage, I'm not going to answer that question in a book. About two years ago, my office location changed to downtown Chicago. My new office space was across the street from my wife's office.

When I started commuting to the city, I drove in. Approximately two months into my new commute, I asked her, "Do *you want to ride in with me?*" She responded, *"What the heck. I'll give it a try."* Initially, I was surprised with the response, but later realized that she joined me because it was raining out and I could drop her off in front of her office opposed to walking multiple city blocks to and from the train station. Now it's been two years and she has never missed a ride. Why did she get out of her old routine? Here is why. The reason is not because it was faster. It was about the same amount of time. Sometimes it would actually be longer because of traffic. It wasn't because it was more convenient. She was now on my schedule, which is anything but a routine. What we found out is that we got what everybody wants more of, and that is TIME.

How did we get more of that finite thing called TIME? As I said, the travel time was not less. We had the same amount of time, but we managed to do more with it. For the half an hour on the way in, we got to talk about what was going on with the family. We did family planning. We talked about the kids, their schooling and activities. Like most others, we have phones and tablets. We had the ability to plan and book vacations. My wife would shop on Amazon, eBay, One Kings Lane just to name a few. That was not necessarily a good thing for me, but she enjoyed the shopping sprees. I would eventually drop her off in front of her office to begin her work day. After my work day, I would call her to set a time to pick her up in front of her building. Then, we would begin the back end of our commute. On our way home, we would pick up ingredients for dinner instead of going back out after we got home. We would talk about our day, which we would usually do in the evening if we had time after running around chasing the kids. It was amazing. If you even think about this, traveling together helped our family communications. We never thought that taking the car in together would actually buy us time. The hour we spent together in the car was an hour we would have spent when we got home from work. It was simple math; we each got an extra hour to do something else. The idea to drive in together happened purely by accident, but my wife had the COURAGE to change her routine and that COURAGE bought us the most precious resource of all, TIME.

One of the dumbest things I ever did also ended up changing my routine. As most know, Chicago gets very cold in the winter time. This means you have two choices. Wear a hat and get hat-head or don't wear a hat and don't get hat-head and freeze. Here is where the accident happened. Last winter, my hair was getting a little long and I needed to get a haircut to get it back to my routine length. It all started off innocently enough. I needed a haircut so I called my barber. I, like most men, don't plan weeks in advance to get my hair cut. When it is time for a trim, we call to get in that day. Well, I called my barber and she was on vacation for two weeks. First of all, what barber takes a two-week vacation? Second, how could they take a vacation on the day I need to get my hair cut? I needed my hair cut NOW. In my mind there was only one thing to do, give myself a self-trim. It seemed simple enough. I found an electric razor in the closet. I put the hair cutting blade on and ran it though my locks. Nothing. No hair got cut. I changed the blade to one that cuts more hair off. Again, nothing. I then switched to the next blade which was supposed to cut off more hair…Oops, I immediately heard an awful noise. It sounded like the garbage disposal chewing up an apple. In this case, the sound was my hair being shredded by my razor. I sheepishly looked in the mirror. I took a huge chunk of hair off. I had a bald spot. What do I do? Did I forget to tell you that I was being filmed the next morning and it was now 7:00 pm? Well, I decided to try to even things out. The disposal sounded again! Houston, we have a problem. To the telephone I go to speed dial any and every barber within driving distance. Let me tell you something. Barber shops are not open at night. I finally found a hair salon and spa in the local mall. I tell them my issue. Once they stopped laughing, they told me to come right down and they would try to help me. I rushed over and burst through the door. I got some funny looks. They all looked at each other. One lady said "I can fix that." Everyone else looked at her like she was nuts. As far as I was concerned, I had nothing to lose. The worst case would be for them to shave my head. For all those follicly-challenged people out there, I apologize for that remark. She attacked my head like an artist attacks a blank canvas. A little here and a little there. Forty-five minutes later, she was done. Not bad. It was cropped tight with three claw marks on one side. It looked like I got attacked by a wolverine. If the camera filmed me from straight on and the right side, I could pull this off. My hair was the shortest it's ever been. It wasn't like Kojak, but it was closing in on it. Twenty-four hours later, I realized it was the best winter haircut I could have ever had. I will probably go with a real short hair cut in the winter for the rest of my life. You know why? Not only didn't I have to brush my hair, I could wear a hat, keep my ears warm and not get hat-head. Winner, winner, chicken dinner!

Here's another chance opportunity that someone had the COURAGE to take that set off a fashion statement that is alive and well 160 years later. In 1853, the California gold rush was in full swing, and everyday supplies were in short supply. Levi Strauss, a 24-year-old German immigrant, left New York for San Francisco with a small supply of dry goods with the intentions of opening a branch of his brother's New York dry goods business. Shortly after his arrival, a prospector wanted to know what Mr. Levi Strauss was selling. When Strauss told him he had rough canvas to use for tents and wagon covers, the prospector said, "You should have brought pants!" Saying he could find a pair strong enough to last, Levi Strauss had the canvas made into waist overalls. The rest is history. Levi Strauss could have continued to sell his canvas for tents and wagon covers, much like many others who had arrived to sell their canvas. Instead Levi Strauss had the COURAGE to get off the beaten path and CREATE something else with his canvas.

Ideas come in many shapes and sizes. You are surrounded with great ideas that just need someone with COURAGE to CREATE something with them. I tell you these stories so you start thinking of the opportunities. Things happen around you every day. Do you have the COURAGE and CREATIVITY to take advantage of those opportunities? If you do, it's imperative to start thinking as a leader, and not as a follower.

I often tell a story of a herd of zebra grazing in an open field. This story has a great deal of synergies with the way money managers work. Let's take a look at money managers in the market today. A money manager typically owns 80% of their benchmark, and with the other 20%, they try to differentiate themselves from the benchmark with the hopes that they will outperform the very same benchmark that they own 80% of. If they are successful, the chances of significantly beating the benchmark is limited because of the number of different securities in their portfolio. History has proven over the years that it is much more likely that they will underperform to their benchmark. A great majority of these managers underperform on an annual basis and only a handful will outperform over a five year period. With such poor performance, why does the industry continue to manage their portfolios this way? The reason they do this is for safety. It is because there is "strength and safety in numbers." If others underperform at the same level, then they believe that they are safe relative to the pack. There is something inherently sick about that logic, but it appears to be a very logical theory in practice today. We, as a society, are followers of the theory of "strength in numbers." One of the best ways I have to debug that theory is to speak of the herd of zebra grazing in the open field. So if you look at a herd of zebras, they always are together in a big herd. Why is that?

Protection! Right? They're there because of protection. They too seem to believe in the theory of "strength in numbers." Now think about it. They stand there and say, *If we stay together we will be better protected from the predators.* Does this strategy work? If the predator attacks, are they all protected? The ones in the middle certainly are, right? At the end of the story, let me know if the zebra in the middle is safest. Let's get back to the story of the zebra grazing. While grazing, the herd moves around as a group. They move in each direction to eat fresh grass. The guys on the inside, they're not getting the fresh grass. The guys on the outside are eating the fresh grass. To the simple theory of "strength is numbers," the safest zebras in the middle eat the trampled down, already grazed grass. The zebras on the outside, which appear to be the most vulnerable, are eating the freshest, non-trampled grass. Here is where the theory starts to fall apart. The zebras on the outside are getting more nourishment, which should make them bigger, stronger, and faster.

So when the predators decide they are hungry, they attack the herd. In all the chaos, what happens to the herd? They scatter. Every zebra for themselves. What happened to the first layer of protection, the zebras on the outside? They are gone. They are thinking survival. They are fleeing the danger as fast as they can.

Who gets caught? The ones who thought they were the safest because they were in the middle of the pack. But the reason they weren't the safest is because they didn't get the fresh grass. They were less nourished and weaker animals. That equals slower. The predators aren't stupid. They're not going to chase down the faster zebras. They are there to eat, not to exercise. They attack the slowest ones they can find. They don't want to overwork to get a little chow.

So if money managers, or society, continue to live inside this herd of safety, they could become prey to the predators. I will argue that the safest place to be is not inside the "strength in numbers" circle, but on the outside where you have the COURAGE to be the leader, with the ability to get bigger, faster and stronger. To flourish in society and business, we need to break away from the pack. We need to be the people on the outside eating the fresh grass.

How do we become the ones outside the pack, the ones eating the fresh grass? We need two things. We need to generate CREATIVE ideas and have the COURAGE to act on them.

Here's a visual. Look at this railroad yard.

Business today is very much like this rail yard. Like trains in the rail yard, we are all trying to get out and move forward. Most cars are happy attaching themselves to other cars and traveling together in the same direction at the same speed. Once again we are talking about "strength or safety in numbers." The leaders are the engines maneuvering around to be the first out of the rail yard. All the tracks in the rail yard eventually converge into one single track. They are all jockeying to be that first car out. How do they do it? What's the smartest way to get out of there? If you had a plan and you're there, what's your strategy?

You are probably thinking logically.

You're not thinking outside the box!

Think outside the box!

Take the damn plane you see in the picture!

The odds are that you were building a strategy to get your train in front of the others. If you were thinking of something other than taking the train, Congratulations! This is where we need CREATIVITY. Doing the same thing better than everyone else is great, but greatness comes from finding a better way to do things.

Be the damn plane. Get outside the box. Don't look and think how does everybody else do it? Ask yourself the question "is there a better way of doing it?" Just because everybody else is doing it the same way, doesn't mean that we have to do it the same way? You want to be on that airplane. You don't want to be sitting there following the rest of the competition. You want the competition to be following you.

So we've got to move outside the box. Right now we, society, tend to live inside the confines of the box. Why do we live inside the box? As we talked about with the herd, Safety!

We believe that we want to be safe. That's the main reason we want to live inside the proverbial box. It's safety versus risk. The whole idea of living outside the box can be scary.

"To live a creative life, we must lose our fear of being wrong" –Joseph Chilton Pearce

"Creativity requires the courage to let go of certainties." –Erich Fromm

"If you're not prepared to be wrong, you'll never come up with anything original." – Sir Kenneth Robinson

We need to have the COURAGE to overcome our fears of being wrong and letting go of certainties. Contrary to popular thinking, I think it's risky to be in the box. I don't think the risk is being outside the box. Following a herd of sheep over a cliff isn't the safest path. We need to stop acting like a herd.

Let's get a little deeper. Let's think about human beings. Humans, as facts would have it, are the only creative species on the planet. Yes, we're the only ones. Other animals, creatures and species create, but they're not creative.

Think about a beaver. A beaver goes out and builds a dam. The dams built are always horizontal dams. Do you ever think Mr. Beaver says, "I have a big family so I think I will build a vertical one," A two story dam makes sense, right? Beavers and all other species except humans can't think that way.

What's the evolution of the dog, the cat, and the zebra? They have never changed. They may create things, but they're not CREATIVE. And the reason why we're the ultimate species is we're CREATIVE. We, as humans, were born to be creative. We need to recognize that CREATIVE feature that we are ALL born with that makes us unique.

The 1980 US Olympic hockey team is something that I always like to refer to because just the mention of that team makes Americans smile. Smiling is good. The main reason for my reference to this team has a lot to do with how we were feeling as a country before those games and how the country's spirit and patriotism were heightened after them. The impact was huge. Going into the Olympics was not a good time for us as a nation. We were coming off of double digit interest rates. Iran had taken over our embassy in Iran and Americans were being held hostage for over a year. We were in the midst of a fuel shortage. Because we were rationing gas, Americans would line up based on their license plate number to get gas. The "Cold War" was in in full swing. The United States was in a bad way with limited hopes of a brighter future. For Americans, other than maybe the Great Depression, this was as bad as it got. If you were around then, you will remember that the mood of the nation was not good. Americans were burning flags. We were not proud to be Americans. History shows how the success of our Olympic team against our "Cold War" enemy, the Soviet Union, helped turn the country around. All of a sudden, we had hope. We remember beating the Soviets, but what most people may not remember is that we were up against a stronger, more talented team with an incredible winning streak. They were the superior team. So why did the Americans win that day? How did we beat that superior team? It boiled down to a coach, Herb Brooks, who did not follow the herd.

Herb took a look at North American hockey. North American hockey was what is known as a "North/South" style. The puck was always moving forward. It was based on "head manning the puck." That was the game that they invented. That was the game that they perfected. There was never a thought of changing their style. It was the Soviets who ignored what the herd was doing and developed a style of hockey now known as "flow hockey." Instead of always "head manning the puck," they were willing to move the puck backwards. If they ran into a barrier that prevented them from moving forward, they would move it backwards and regroup. In North America, if we ran into a barrier that prevented us from moving forward, we would shoot the puck down the ice and go fight to get it back. In other words, we were willing to lose the puck with the hope that we could fight to win it back. The Soviets didn't believe in turning the puck over and fighting for it. They wanted to keep possession of the puck even if it meant going backwards. The Soviet system proved to be the superior system. The North Americans were not willing to change their style. We were the herd.

Herb Brooks changed that. He got CREATIVE. He changed the game. He changed the way the North Americans played the game. It wasn't easy. The entire US Hockey Association leaders were up in arms. He didn't pick the best players for the team. He picked the best players that would fit into his new system. He was heavily criticized. He knew that the Soviets had built a system to take advantage of the way their competitors played, but no one had ever thought of what it would take to beat the Soviet style. The Soviets knew that their competition would always be defensive minded. Their competition was designed to stop the Soviets from scoring. Brooks decided to change things. Instead of being defensive, he designed his own flow style that was more offensive. The Soviets had never seen this style. Herb Brooks' best defense was a good offense. This style confused the Soviets. Eventually self-doubt started to creep into the minds of the Soviet players and coaches. They started to make uncharacteristic mistakes. If you saw the movie, Miracle, you know how it ends. What really happened was the best team didn't win that day. CREATIVITY won. CREATIVITY turned this country around.

If you start looking at successful teams, or successful firms, or successful people, they all have a CREATIVITY gene. It's the

CREATIVITY that makes them special. It's the CREATIVIITY that sets them apart from everybody else, from the herd. You start talking about the Steve Jobs of this world, the Alexander Graham Bells, and the Thomas Edison's, you start talking about people who have done something special; it's because they have been CREATIVE.

To do something special requires us to think outside-of-the-box.

So we need to start innovating. We need to get CREATIVE. So I'm going to give you a little test here.

By the age of 40, adults are 3% as creative as they were at the age of 7.

True or False?

That's true.

Adults are 3% as creative as a 7 year old! That's crazy, but it is reality.

Creativity and IQ are unrelated.

True or False?

True.

IQ has nothing to do with creativity.

*Most people use 15%
of their brain power.*

True or False?

That is false.

Typically we use 2-3% of our brain power. The only person that came close was Albert Einstein and they say he only used 10% of his brain power. Clearly, we're not taxing our mental capacity.

Some people are born with a creative gene and some are not.

True or False?

That is absolutely false.

Everybody is born with it.

*Creativity skipped me
a long time ago.*

True or False?

That one's on you.

So what is the real reason we've lost CREATIVITY? Go back to your days in kindergarten or nursery school. They put us in groups, gave us finger paints, blocks. We were taught to be CREATIVE. We were taught to use our imaginations. We were exercising our CREATIVITY. For the first 7-8 years of our lives we are very, very CREATIVE. Then what happened? We entered first grade. They put us in desks. We sat there. The teacher sat in front of the class and lectured us. There was no longer CREATIVITY and imagination. There was right and wrong. It was typical learning. If you're going to do a seminar or presentation, everybody sits in the audience facing forward towards the speaker (teacher), the speaker speaks at them and everybody listens to the speaker. Since first grade, that is how we learned and we continue to learn that way. We have had the CREATIVITY taught out of us as a society.

School decides to cut costs, what's the first thing that goes?

Art and Music! We gave away the CREATIVITY. We cut CREATIVITY out of the budget.

I, for one believe that our educational system is at fault. Learning has become a routine. We cut CREATIVITY out of the budget. If you think about it, the students that have learned and retained the most are perfectly trained to be professors. I am certainly not an authority in this field, but many who are have said similar things.

Sir Kenneth Robinson is an advisor on education and a renowned speaker on how we have educated CREATIVITY out of people.

I have translated a clip from one of his presentations.

"So I want to talk about education. And I want to talk about creativity. My contention is that creativity now is as important in education as literacy. And we should treat it with the same status.

I heard a great story recently. I love telling it, of a little girl who was in a drawing lesson. She was six. She was in the back drawing, and the teacher said, this little girl hardly ever paid attention, but in this drawing lesson she did.

The teacher was fascinated. She went over to her and said. "What are you drawing?" And the girl said, "I'm drawing a picture of God." The teacher said, but nobody knows what God looks like." And the girl said, "They will in a minute."

When my son was four in England, actually he was 4 everywhere to be honest. If we're being strict about it, he was 4 everywhere that year. He was in the nativity play. Do you remember the story?

It's a big, big story. Mel Gibson did the sequel. You may have seen it. Nativity II.

But James got the part of Joseph, which we were thrilled about. We believed this to be one of the lead parts. We had the place crammed full of agents and t-shirts printed "James Robinson IS Joseph." He didn't have to speak, but you know the bit where the 3 kings come in?

They come in bearing gifts. And they bring gold, and gifts. We're sitting there, and they, I think, just went out of sequence. Because we talked a little while afterwards and said, you okay with that? James said "Yeah, why? Was something wrong?"

They just switched. Anyways, the three boys come in. Little 4-year-olds with tea towels on their heads walk in. And they put these boxes down. And the first boy said, "I bring you gold."

And the second boy said, "I bring you myrrh."

And the third boy said, "Frank sent this."

What these things have in common is that kids will take a chance. If they don't know, they'll have a go. They're not frightened of being wrong.

Now I don't mean to say that being wrong is the same thing as being creative. What we do know is if you're not prepared to be wrong, you'll never come up with anything original.

And by the time they get to be adults, most kids have lost that capacity. They have become frightened of being wrong. And we run our companies like this. We stigmatize mistakes. And we're now running national education systems where mistakes are the worst thing you can make. And the result is that we are educating people out of their creative capacities.

Picasso once said that all children are born artists. The problem is to remain an artist as we grow up. I believe this passionately - we don't grow into creativity, we grow out of it, or rather we get educated out of it.

So why is this? I lived in Stratford on Avon until about 5 years ago. In fact we moved from Stratford to Los Angeles. So you can imagine what a seamless transition this was.

Actually, we lived in a place called Smitherfield just outside Stratford, which is where Shakespeare's father was born. Are you struck by a new thought? I was.

You don't think of Shakespeare having a father, do you? Did you ever think of Shakespeare being a child? Shakespeare being seven years old?

I never thought of it. He was in somebody's English class, wasn't he?

How annoying would that be?

What would you think, I must try harder?

Being sent to bed by his dad. Go to bed now, to William Shakespeare. And put the pencil down. And stop speaking like that. It's confusing everybody.

Anyway, we moved from Stratford to Los Angeles. And I just want to say a word about the transition. My son didn't want to come. I've got 2 kids. He's 21 now, and my daughter's 16. He didn't want to come to Los Angeles. He loved it, but he had a girlfriend in England. This was the love of his life. Sarah.

He'd known her for a month. Mind you, they'd had their 4th anniversary by then, because it's a long time when you're 16.

Anyway, he was really upset on the plane. He said," I'll never find another girl like Sarah." And we were rather pleased about that, frankly, because she was the main reason we were leaving the country. But something strikes you when you move to America and when you travel around the world. Every education system on earth has the same hierarchy of subjects. Every one. It doesn't matter where you go. You think it would be otherwise, but it isn't. At the top are mathematics and languages. Then there are the humanities. And at the bottom are the arts, everywhere on earth.

And in pretty much every system too, there's a hierarchy within the arts. Art and music are normally given a higher status in schools than drama and dance. There isn't an education system on the planet that teaches dance every day to children the way we teach them mathematics.

Why not? I think this is rather important. I think math is very important, but so is dance. Children dance all the time if they're allowed to. We all do. We all have bodies. Don't we?

Truthfully what happens is as our children grow up we start to educate them progressively from the waist up, and then we focus on their heads, and slightly to one side. If you were to visit education as an alien and say, "what's it for?" Public education. I think you'd have to conclude if you look at the output. Who really succeeds by this? Who does everything they should? Who gets all the brownie points? Who are the winners? I think you'd have to conclude the whole purpose of public education throughout the world is to produce university professors.

They're the people who come out the top. And I used to be one. So there!

And I like university professors. But we shouldn't hold them up as the high water mark of all human achievement. They're just a form of life. Another form of life. But they're rather curious, and I say this out of affection for them.

There's something curious about them. And in my experience, not all of them, but typically they live in their heads. They live up there and slightly to one side. They're disembodied in a kind of a literal way. They hook up their bodies as a form of transport for their heads.

It's a way of getting their head to meetings. If you want real evidence of out of body experiences, get yourself along to a residential conference of a scene of academics. And pop into the discothèque on the final night. And there you'll see it. Grown men and women writhing uncontrollably off the beat, waiting for it to end so they can go home and write a paper about it.

Now our education system is predicated upon the idea of academic ability. And there's a reason. The whole system was invented around the world. There were no systems of public education really before the 19th century. They all came into being to meet the needs of industrialism.

So the hierarchy is rooted in two ideas. 1) the most useful subjects for work are at the top. So you were probably steered benignly away from things, as a kid, you liked on the grounds you would never get a job doing that. Is that right? Don't do music. You're not going to be a musician. Don't do art. You won't be an artist. Benign advice.

Now profoundly mistaken. The whole world is engulfed in revolution.

2) Academic ability has really come to dominate our view of intelligence, because the universities designed the system in their image. If you think of it, the whole system of public education around the world is a protracted system of university entrance. And the consequence is that many highly-talented, brilliant, creative people think they're not.

Because the thing they were good at in school wasn't valued or was actually stigmatized.

And I think we can't afford to go on that way."

So I understand that's a long story, but it makes you think. It's going to make you think that we've always been thinking the exact same way.

In 2013, Daniel Luzer wrote an article titled "What Kills Creativity?" Luzer says " Many American writers fear that standardized testing could destroy our children. They might be right."

In the article Luzer writes, "More than 120 American writers, including Judy Blume, Lee Bennett Hopkins, and Donald Crews, as well as National Book Award winners Kathryn Erkine and Philip Hoose sent an open letter to the White House warning President Obama that the increasing use of standardized tests in American schools are destroying creativity and undermining "children's love of reading and literature. ...requirements to evaluate teachers based on student test scores impose more standardized exams and crowd out exploration."

American children are spending too much time on test prep and "too little time curling up with books that fire their imaginations," the writers concluded."

It is clear that there is a growing concern that CREATIVITY is being thwarted by standardized testing and the methods used to teach our kids in the American public school system.

We've been educated into thinking the same way. If we keep thinking that way, we are going to stay in our rut. We need to bring that CREATIVITY out. If we want to innovate, we need to bring that back. We need CREATIVITY to be innovators. So how do you innovate?

How do you generate an idea? Steve Jobs said "innovation distinguishes between a leader and a follower." He's absolutely right. We cannot follow if we want to succeed in this business. We want to be the best, we want to be the person that takes the airplane and gets out in front. We need to lead.

So often I hear from people that they don't like their jobs, or they are unmotivated. If you think about how productive you or your colleagues are, you would be amazed how little production people get done. Most professionals that track actual "engaged" work hours find that people typically work 15-20 hours of a 40 hour work week. The other time is spent chatting, eating and procrastinating. I find that mind boggling. Why is that? Why the lack of productivity?

The level of people's production is closely correlated with what I call "intrinsic motivation." "Intrinsic motivation" is the passion for what you are doing. The key word is passion. If you have passion for what you are doing, you are always engaged. This also rings true at work, marriage, hobbies and life.

There is so much outside involvement that goes into being intrinsically motivated. If you are forced into a routine, feel that no one will listen to your ideas, or there are no avenues to make positive change for the future, you will be less engaged and less productive. You, like most, will put in your 15-20 productive hours per week.

What makes you more productive is the CREATIVITY card. If you feel that you can create, present ideas, change or improve things at work you will be motivated to work harder and be a leader.

Take a moment to think about your passions. What is your love? Is there something in your life that you love to do? That love or passion might be a hobby, family or work. Whatever it is, it is what you devote a great deal of time pursuing and brings you the most satisfaction. It is that passion, or "intrinsic motivation," that drives extreme production in that passion.

It is my experience that the most productive people in business are business owners. These people are typically passionate about their firms. That is because they are the one's making the decisions, guiding the course of the firm. Every day, they are thinking what they can do to make their firm better. They are thinking CREATIVELY. Every day they are challenging themselves. They are controlling their own destiny. They are passionate and have "intrinsic motivation."

Others that exhibit "intrinsic motivation" are those who are given the freedom and opportunity to influence the direction of the firm, department, product, etc. In the business that I am in, I have a small army of people that all have similar responsibilities to accomplish a set goal. Most of my competitors have similar goals. These firms typically institute very rigid methods to accomplish the task. I have observed, and even worked at many of these firms. I know from my research and firsthand experience that they are very organized, methodical, track-able, and functional. They motivate through compensation. Compensation certainly can motivate, but can also demotivate. At some point they "expect" their compensation to grow. If the compensation stagnates or declines at any point it can be very disappointing and demotivating.

Passion and "intrinsic motivation" is the driving tool that never falters. If people feel involved, important and have the ability to be heard they will be more productive. How do you "institute" passion and "intrinsic motivation" in a work force? The answer is relatively simple...encourage their abilities to make change, tap into their skills, ability, drive and CREATIVITY. A different and fresh perspective can always be advantageous. Human resources are powerful and should be encouraged. The next great idea may come from that rookie who has never spent a day in our business. Don't restrict or shoot down ideas. Ideas are what drive great businesses. Use all resources available!

I have been fortunate enough throughout my career to be a top sales person, manager and owner. Over the years, I have started to ask the question "why have I had such success compared to others?" If you were to ask people who know me well why I am successful, they would point out that I approach things differently than my competitors. I often say "truly successful people are either extraordinary or out-of-the-ordinary." I have chosen the "out-of-the-ordinary" route. The reason for going in this direction dates back to my school years.

I often tell people that being CREATIVE comes easy to me. I believe I have an advantage over most. I am very dyslexic. Reading and comprehension is very difficult for me. All my early testing, forms of IQ testing, say I should be tops in my class at school. That never happened. School did not come easy to me. If reading was involved, I struggled. It was natural for me to migrate to the athletic fields and the arts. I spent most of my academic time exercising the right side of my brain. I was passionate about art, and still am today. In the more mainstream subjects, I would use all my CREATIVE skills to get out of class and assignments. I just prayed that I would get a C. I felt if I went to class, got help from my teachers and they saw I was trying, they would be kind enough to pass me. When I went to college, I took the required classes. Those didn't necessarily go well. I convinced many of my teachers to give me a passing grade. I showed up to every class, sat in the front and asked for extra help. The extra help sessions allowed me to plead the case of "this class is difficult for me but I am trying." Most of these professors were kind and caring and followed the plan and handed me the C. Some were not as kind. Once I got the required classes out of the way it allowed me to get back to my Art class. Art and Art History were a comfort zone and got me a college degree. Majoring in Art is probably not what everyone wants for their kid in college. Luckily, I had great parents who allowed me to pursue an Art major. My dad made me a deal. If I spent the summer working on the floor of the New York Stock Exchange, and learned that business, he would allow me to major in Art. Having parents who let me choose my own path was important. Not many of my friends' parents would have allowed this with their kids. I thank my parents for supporting me and my art (known as being an "artsy fartsy" to my dad).

Once I graduated, I was equipped to excel in business. Most of the other graduates entered into the work force with similar skills. They were well read, well trained and ready to follow a path. For me, I was well trained to blaze my own path. Why was I going to blaze my own path? If I followed the well-traveled path, I would have to "out-extraordinary" them. Because of my learning disability, no matter how hard I worked, I would never excel in their sand box. My only chance to succeed would have to be to take the path less traveled. That strategy worked. I had the advantage. For all the personal hardships my learning disability caused, it turned out to be my asset.

There is a long and distinguished list of successful dyslexic's that have had huge success.

In an article written by Alison Griswold and Dylan Love in "Business Insider" titled "17 Business Titans Who Overcame Dyslexia" they write "Does dyslexia come with hidden advantages?

It is counterintuitive – dyslexia is, after all, classified as a learning disability – but it's a central question in Malcolm Gladwell's new book, David and Goliath.

Gladwell proposes that some of the world's most accomplished people succeeded precisely because of this disability. "Dyslexia – in the best cases – forces you to develop skills that might otherwise have lain dormant," he writes. "It also forces you to do things you might otherwise never have considered."

One of those dyslexic business leaders is Richard Branson. In the article they write about Richard Branson. They write, "The wealthy head of the Virgin Group dropped out of school when he was 16, in large part because of his dyslexia. "My teachers thought I was lazy," he wrote of his experience. But the condition that hurt him in academics helped him as he was building his business. He would ask that all marketing materials be read aloud to him, and assessed them by simplicity and how easy they were to understand. "Over the years, my different way of thinking helped me build the Virgin Group and contributed greatly to our success," Branson reflects. "My dyslexia guided the way we communicate with customers."

Other people sited in the article were Charles Schwab, Ted Turner, Tommy Hilfiger, Bill Hewlett, John Reed, John Chambers, Nancy Brinker, Ingvar Kamprad, Henry Ford, Craig McCaw, O.D. McFee, Paul Orfalea, Bill Samuels Jr., David Neelman, Gary Cohn and David Boies.

All of these people were forced to use their CREATIVITY to overcome their disability. Perhaps they all had an advantage over the masses after all.

Just because that's the way it's always been done doesn't mean it's the best or only way to do it. So we have to start generating ideas. Those dyslexic business leaders have proven that a different path can be successful.

Everybody understands an idea. CREATIVITY is not always making something new. CREATIVITY is often taking two other ideas or innovations and putting them together to form a new idea. CREATIVITY as a mathematical equation:

$$C = P + K + I$$

What is Innovation? CREATIVITY = Person + Knowledge + Information. If you start thinking about that, you (the person) have the knowledge and the information of everything that goes on in your business. How do you take that information, that knowledge, and make a difference?

Think about all the great ideas out there. Where do you think the iPhone came from? Two formally known ideas - a simple cell phone and a personal computer. Wish I had thought of that, right?

How about blue jeans? Where did that come from during the gold rush? They had an abundance of tent canvas and a shortage of sturdy work pants. Some guy by the name of Levi Strauss decides to take that tent canvas and make pants out of them. Thus, the blue jean. Tent canvas plus pants equals blue jeans.

What's pizza? It's bread plus spaghetti sauce.

Think about almost everything you consume or use. It's two formerly known ideas that made it into one. You don't have to reinvent the wheel. Trust me; I'm sure the wheel came from two ideas. It's not that hard to do.

The problem we have is that we have forgotten how to be CREATIVE. We have this muscle that has gone dormant. We can get it back. If you were to going to run a marathon, you would train. You wouldn't go from a couch potato to run the race without training. The same holds true for exercising your CREATIVE muscle.

CREATIVITY in business is a real currency. Everybody has the ability to create, but few use it in business. We typically show up to work at the same time every day prepared to do the same thing every day, and then we leave the job at the same time every day. Our minds are trained to do that. We were not born to be drones. We were trained to be drones. We are in a rut. When we were born, we were innately creative. Over the years, our CREATIVITY has been suppressed. We need to bring that inner

CREATIVITY that is in ALL of us back. It won't just re-appear. We need to train to get it back.

You have to look at this like you are training for a triathlon. When you train for a triathlon you set a schedule to be ready on a specific day. You set your training schedule accordingly to be prepared on that day to compete. Your body is prepared. If you never trained for a triathlon and you were to participate in one tomorrow, the chances are you would not even show up to the race. If you did show up, chances are things would not go well. Heck, at the very least you would probably pull a few muscles.

Your brain is the same way. If we were asked to be CREATIVE today, you probably would ignore the thought and go back to what you do every day. If we did attempt to be CREATIVE, we wouldn't be at our peak CREATIVITY.

It is necessary for us to train our brain to compete and to be CREATIVE. Remember, CREATIVITY is a currency in the business world. The race is scheduled…let's start training.

I have prepared a number of exercises for you to train your brain to be CREATIVE again. I would suggest doing one training exercise per day to get your CREATIVITY back in shape.

Have the COURAGE to CREATE.

CHAPTER 2

Creativity Exercises

"I can't understand why people are frightened of
new ideas. I'm frightened of the old ones."
John Cage, composer

What is another meaning for that sign?

For most of us, we have taken a written road test to get our driver's license. One of the things we needed to learn was the meaning of street signs. Many street signs are just illustrations with no words. It could be swerves in the road, no parking, intersection, do not enter, etc.

Your exercise is to think about other meanings that street signs may have. When you see a street sign ask yourself, "what are alternative meanings to that traffic sign? **WARNING...DON'T FORGET TO KEEP YOUR EYES ON THE ROAD.!**

"You can't keep bitch-slapping your creativity,
or it will run away and find a new pimp."
George Meyer, producer and writer

Communicate...Old School!

In today's age of technology, we have numerous ways to communicate. Think about how you communicate to your clients and colleagues. You have telephone, intercom, email, internet, intranet, social media, etc. What would happen if you needed to communicate with clients and colleagues but the power went out for days? Let's go a step further. What if you couldn't leave your desk? You are confined to your desk and have no electricity.

Your exercise is to imagine living in this scenario. How would you build a communication system for you and your office? How would you communicate back and forth with your teammates? I know the obvious answer would be to yell, but eventually you would lose your voice. **GO FORTH AND COMMUNICATE.**

"The best way to have a good idea is to have lots of ideas."
Linus Pauling

Coffee is not coffee...it is a tomato

Our minds are trained to recognize objects and give them a name. We see a desk and we recognize and call it a desk. We see a telephone and we recognize and call it a telephone. Look around you and name all the objects you can see.

Your exercise is to look at all those objects and give them new names. You now recognize and rename that desk as a giraffe. The phone may now be an orchid. How many objects can you rename before you run out of names? Every day for a week play this game. You should see the number of renamed objects increase daily. Instead of waking up and getting a cup of coffee out of the coffee pot, wake up and get a box of tomato out of the tomato screen. **ENJOY THE TOMATO.**

"Follow the path of the unsafe, independent thinker.
Expose your ideas to the dangers of controversy. Speak
your mind and fear less the label of 'crackpot' than the
stigma of conformity. And on issues that seem important
to you, stand up and be counted at any cost."
Thomas J. Watson, past CEO of IBM

Your name is a Picasso

A letter or number is more than a letter or a number. It is a creative form. Some could say they are artistic forms. Look at the letters and numbers differently. Flip them around. Turn them inside out. Change their shape and form. Turn them into artistic forms.

Your exercise is to take your full name and turn it into an artistic form. Flip the letters around, change the fonts, change the style, and change the colors. Turn your name into a piece of art. How beautiful can you make your name? **CREATE YOUR OWN PICASSO.**

"A simple idea can, inspire, motivate, and produce change."

"A good traveler is one who knows how
to travel with their mind."
Michael Bassey Johnson, poet, playwright and novelist

You may be the next Armani

Your desk is your desk. You were probably assigned or given your desk. Perhaps you picked out your own desk. Regardless, take a good look at your desk. How functional is it? Is the space, shape and size optimal? How are the power sources? Is it attractive? Is it comfortable?

Your exercise is to design your own desk/work space. Don't design it in your mind…put it on paper. Design it like you are a Desk Engineer. Be creative and functional. Draw it up so a manufacturer could understand the drawing well enough to build it. **YOU COULD BECOME THE NEXT ARMANI OF OFFICE FURNITURE.**

"Ideas are the factors that lift civilization. They create revolutions. There is more dynamite in an idea than in many bombs."

Bishop Vincent

"The true sign of intelligence is not
knowledge but imagination."
Albert Einstein

Should Saturday really be Saturday?

Back in 400 AD in Rome, the Romans adopted the seven days in a week idea. It eventually spread to Europe and then the rest of the world. The name of each day was related to Roman mythology. It is over 1600 years since the adoption of those names. The world has changed so it is time to rename the days to fit our times.

Your exercise is to rename the days of the week. They can have a theme or be loosely connected. The names can be any size and can mean anything. Perhaps you invent new words and names. The only requirement is that each day ends with the suffix "-day."

BE THE PERSON THAT CHANGES THE CALENDAR FOR THE NEXT 1600 YEARS.

"Great minds discuss ideas. Average minds discuss events. Small minds discuss people."
Henry Thomas Buckle

62

Who's your league?

Professional sports leagues usually have logos that are two or three colors with a silhouette of a player or ball with negative space.

Your exercise is to design your own logo for a sports league participating in these activities:

Pizza Eating
Wind Surfing
Gardening
Grocery Shopping
Internet Surfing

WHAT'S YOUR LOGO?

"Imagination is more important than knowledge."
Albert Einstein

Extraordinary or "Out-of-the-Ordinary?"

I have always said "the most successful people in business are either extraordinary or out-of-the-ordinary." What I mean by extraordinary people are people who are better at a particular aspect of the something. If your industry is focusing on service, there is usually someone or some firm that is better than the rest at it. These people and firms are extraordinary and everyone is chasing them. The other very successful person or firm looks at what everyone else is doing and finds a different road to travel. They do the "out-of-the-ordinary." Think about the airline industry many years ago. All the airlines were concentrating their efforts on improving their services. They were offering more and more. They were all trying to "keep up with the Joneses." Southwest Airlines did the "out-of-the-ordinary." They went the opposite way and cut out the frills and offered cheap fares. That differentiation made them very successful. Now, the airline industry keeps a keen eye on Southwest and what they will come up with next. Sometimes, just doing the opposite is all you need to do to find success. Instead of adding services, cut out the frills and lower the price. That might be what the consumers crave.

Your exercise is to write down five things that everyone in your industry does, the things that every firm is focused on improving, and then do the opposite. If you did the opposite, how could that help you? Write down the pros of doing the opposite. Are you on to anything? **OPPOSITES CAN ATTRACT.**

"You can never solve a problem on the
level on which it was created."
Albert Einstein

Bring back that idea

Thomas Edison once said, "Many of life's failures are people who did not realize how close they were to success when they gave up."

Your exercise is to list five ideas in your life that you gave up on. Bring them back to life and see where they might take you.

BRING THOSE IDEAS BACK TO LIFE.

"Creativity involves breaking out of established patterns
in order to look at things in a different way."
Edward de Bono

It ain't as simple as you think

Sometimes we take for granted some of the simplest things. There are things that we do every day that we take for granted. Have you ever thought about how you tie the laces to your shoes or button your shirt?

Your exercise is to write detailed instructions on how you tie the laces of your shoes. **DON'T GET YOURSELF KNOTTED UP**.

"The difficulty lies not so much in developing
new ideas as escaping from old ones."
John Maynard Keynes

Where is X?

Do you know where everything is in your office or work space? Do you know where every letter is in your space? I'm not talking about letters that you send or received in the mail or electronically. I'm talking about the alphabet.

Your exercise is to use your cell phone or camera to take a picture of every letter in the alphabet that you can find in your work space. No two letters can come from the same object. **WARNING..."X" ISN'T EASY TO FIND.**

"Creativity can solve almost any problem. The creative art,
the defeat of habit by originality, overcomes everything."
George Lois, art director, designer and author

That was my idea

Have you ever had an idea and someone else had the same idea, but they followed through on it and made a lot of money? The answer is probably yes. I call these "Million Dollar Ideas" that got away from me. There are two important things to learn here. Produce as many "Million Dollar Ideas" as you can and act on those "Million Dollar Ideas."

Your exercise is to put together a running list of all your "Million Dollar Ideas." Also go around to all you colleagues and friends and ask them to add to your list. If you and your pals know that an idea that can make you grossly rich is one idea away, your mind will create numerous ideas. **GET GROSSLY RICH.**

"It's easy to attack and destroy an act of creation.
It's a lot more difficult to perform one."
Chuck Palahniuk, novelist

Burst the Barrier!

Fear of being wrong will prevent you from achieving greatness. Many people put up barriers to protect themselves from being wrong. Most of the people do this. If you want to achieve greatness you need to get past these mental and physical barriers. Every day we see physical barriers to prevent things from happening outside those barriers. We also have mental barriers that prevent us from stepping out of our comfort zone to create something new and different. We need to get past those physical and mental barriers.

Your exercise is to take pictures of physical barriers around you that prohibit "something" from happening. This could be an executive assistant, acting as the gatekeeper to the president of your firm. Wouldn't the President like to hear your great idea? Also write down mental barriers that prevent you from exploring new ideas. Take 10 physical or mental pictures and think about why they protect or prohibit you. Once you know if that barrier protects or prohibits you, then you will be ready to burst through those barriers. **NOTHING SHOULD GET IN YOUR WAY TO GREATNESS.**

"I never made one of my discoveries through
the process of rational thinking"
Albert Einstein

Let the games begin

If you are like me and many others, you grew up loving sports. As a youth I would play sports whenever I could. I would still love to live that lifestyle, but this thing called a job gets in the way. Now, I only have time to play after work. How could I change that so I could play at work?

Your exercise is to invent a sport that you can play at your desk with objects that you have in your area. Dream up the game and write the rules and regulations of your new sport. Maybe it will be an Olympic event someday. **LET THE GAMES BEGIN.**

"Imagination is everything. It is the
preview of life's attractions."
Albert Einstein

I hear you

I love James Bond movies. One of my favorite parts of these movies is when they roll out the new gadgets. What are your favorite 007 gadgets? Weather it is a jetpack in "Thunderball," a portable gyrocopter in "You Only Live Twice," or the laser piston gun in "Golden Eye," he is always equipped with cool devices. It would be awesome if we could have his cool gadgets.

Your exercise is to design your own gadget designed to spy on your competitions board meetings. What would the gadget look like, what would it be able to do? How do you control it? Just think how much we could learn about our competition if we had this Spy gadget. Design it and draw it up. **THERE ARE NO SECRETS.**

"All achievements, all earned riches, have their beginning in an idea."

Napoleon

"I like to listen. I have learned a great deal from
listening carefully. Most people never listen."
Ernest Hemmingway

I always do that

Over the years, we have become creatures of habit. We have developed routines. Why have we developed these routines? Many professionals would say it is for safety. If we do the same thing every day, there is the safety of knowing the outcome. Think about your routines. You wake up for work at the same time. You have a very structured routine to get dressed and get out of your house to go to work. You take the same route to work. You get your cup of coffee at the same place. You get to work at the same time. You get the idea. We are creatures of routines. The problem is routines stifle creativity.

Your exercise is to write down 15 things, routines, you do every day. Think about why you do each one of them. Now, think about how you can break those routines. Now do it! Take a different route to and from work. Get your coffee from somewhere else, etc. Open your mind to different ideas. **DON'T GET STIFLED BY ROUTINES.**

"Creativity takes courage."

"The only constant in our business is that everything is changing. We have to take advantage of change and not let it take advantage of us. We have to be ahead of the game."
Michael Dell

What is in the logo?

A logo should be designed to identify with the brand. Some are very successful, most are not. A logo should allow the user to have an idea of what business they are in just by their logo. Can you identify logos that are identifiable to a business?

Your exercise is to have a friend or colleague cut out logos from magazines. Make sure the logo doesn't have the company name on it. Also, have them write the name of the company and their industry on the back of the logo. I want you to do two things. First, without reading the back of the logo, can you identify the business they are in? Two, take the logos that you cannot identify with and read what industry they are in. Redesign their logo to be more identifiable with their industry. **BE A DESIGNER.**

"Where all think alike, no one thinks very much."

Walter Lippmann

"If you want to increase your success
rate, double your failure rate."
Thomas J Watson, Founder of IBM

It's just a brick

I look at rocks differently these days. You may look at a rock as just another object. Usually we are trying to move or remove rocks. They are often getting in our way. They are a nuisance. A few years ago, a guy came up with the silliest idea that made him a fortune. Take a little rock, name it, stick it in a box and call it a "Pet Rock." Are you kidding me? No, I'm not kidding you. One Christmas it was the big seller. Some creative guy took this simple rock and found a different use for it and made a fortune.

Your exercise is to take a brick and think on 50 things you can do with that brick. You will probably start with building a house, wall, walkway and driveway. After that you will get creative. **MAYBE YOU WILL HAVE THE NEXT PET ROCK.**

"An unhatched idea is nothing more than just
another idea that dies on the vine."
Michael Balch

Hatch an idea

We often explain new ideas by associating them with old ideas. We think in metaphors. It makes sense; people struggle to understand a completely new concept. The military loves to give metaphoric names to their weapons. Think about the army designing a missile that is capable of seeking out heat from an enemy vehicle and attacking it. Instead of explaining how it works, just give it a name that people can identify with. There is a snake, called a sidewinder that detects the heat of their prey and attacks it. It's no coincidence that the heat seeking missile is called the "Sidewinder." It is no coincidence that the bomb that gets dropped in the mountains of Afghanistan to clear foliage and vegetation, for the purpose of creating landing zones for helicopters, is called a "Daisy Cutter."

Your exercise is to find 10 things in your house or office and develop a metaphor for them. **"BROOD" OVER THE EXERCISE AND "HATCH" A GREAT METAPHOR.**

"The chief enemy
of creativity is
good sense."

Pablo Picasso

"You can't use up creativity. The more you use, the more you have."

Maya Angelou, poet, author, dancer, actress and singer

"Creativity requires the courage to let go of certainties."

Erich Fromm, psychologist and Author

"Creativity is contagious. Pass it on."
Albert Einstein

Mission Impossible

Our world is ever changing. There are advances being made every day. Technology, for one, is moving and changing at break neck speeds. Think about how all these changes have affected you and your business.

Your exercise is to look around your business, or your home, and think about if you could make the impossible possible. Come up with an invention that would help you. Just a few years ago people would have never thought of driving and walking around talking on the cell phone. The personal computer was a complete game changer. What would you invent that would change your life. With your new invention, how would it affect your life? Would it make it better or make other things more complicated? **MAKE THE IMPOSSIBLE POSSIBLE.**

"Thank goodness I was never sent to school; it would have rubbed off some of the originality."

Beatrix Potter, Author

"Ideas are like rabbits. You get a couple and learn how to handle them, and pretty soon you have a dozen."
John Steinbeck, author

Where did that word come from?

Have you ever thought about who and how words are invented? Who came up with the word computer, tire, chair, car or apple? If you are a Latin scholar, you can build words using Latin meanings. But, who invented all those Latin words? Think of all the words in the dictionary. Where did they come from and what went into making them words?

Your exercise is to take something you know and change the word. It can be something you use every day or a project that you are working on. You can invent an entirely new word, combine two or more existing words or use your Latin education to describe your new word. **BE A WORDSMITH.**

"Imitation is suicide."
Ralph Waldo Emerson

Where do ideas come from?

As I wrote earlier in this book, an idea is often taking two known ideas and combining them into on new idea. Did Steve Jobs think a cell phone and a personal computer combined would be a great idea? Probably. I'm sure it wasn't an accident. There are so many things we touch every day that are a combination of two known ideas that combined into a new idea. Think about what they are.

Your exercise is to invent a new product. Can you think of two things, or items, that you know and combine them into one new idea? Start with one new idea. Don't stop there. Keep combining old ideas. Before you know it, you may have the next iPhone. **BE THE NEXT STEVE JOBS.**

"If we could only pull out our brain and use only our eyes."

Pablo Picasso

"Creativity is the power to connect
the seemingly unconnected."
William Plomer, author

Break the status quo

Humans tend to conform to the status quo. As I stated earlier in this book, humans like routines. The "status quo," routine, is safe and comfortable. How many times do you get annoyed with the status quo and don't do anything about it.

Your exercise is to write down ten things that you do every day that bug you or your clients. After you write the list of ten things that annoy you and/or your clients, try to CREATE a new way to solve the annoyance. This should help make your life and business a little bit better. **STOP BEING ANNOYED.**

"Creativity is as important as literacy."
Sir Kenneth Robinson, author, speaker, advisor on education

Don't flop

Many times knowledge gets in our way. Albert Einstein once said, "Imagination is more important than knowledge." We often think that just because we have been doing things the same way for years that it must be the correct way. Prior to 1968, the conventional way to jump over the bar of the high jump in the Olympics was either to dive over head first or hurdle the bar. That was the common thought for over a century. Prior to the 1968 Olympics, a medical student, Dick Fosbury, researched the human body and came up with a thought that the best way to jump over a high bar was not to dive or hurdle, but it was to jump over with his back to the bar. It later became known as the "Fosbury Flop." Not only did the new method win him the gold medal in 1968, but it revolutionized the sport.

Your exercise is to build a presentation on how to ignore existing knowledge. It sounds simple, but it is not. **LOSE ALL EXISTING KNOWLEDGE.**

"To live a creative life, we must lose our fear of being wrong."

Joseph Chilton Pearce, Author

"Courage is what it takes to stand up and speak;
courage is also what it takes to sit down and listen.
Winston Churchill

Find that needle

A good idea isn't always the best idea. When people sit around and try to solve a problem, or find a solution, they often accept the first good idea. Great problem solvers and creative people don't stop with the first answer. They push on to see if they can find a better solution. Truly successful people never stop trying to improve on ideas. Albert Einstein was asked, "What is the difference between you and the rest of us?" He replied, "If you are asked to look for a needle in a haystack, then you search until you find it, whereas I search until I find all the needles."

Your exercise is to push to find a better solution. The next time you're in a meeting with people and trying to find a solution, be the person that doesn't automatically agree with a good solution. See if you can make that solution better. People will probably get annoyed with you, but they will learn to respect a better solution.

LOOK FOR ALL THE NEEDLES IN THE HAYSTACK.

"Creativity arises from our ability to see things from many different angles."

Keri Smith, Author

"Only those who will risk going too far can
possibly find out how far one can go."
T.S. Elliot

Does an idea stand a chance?

In today's day and age, it is so difficult to get an idea through. So often an idea gets criticized or ridiculed in front of your peers. This thwarts the chances of presenting another idea. This has been going on since the beginning of time. Every day, people's creative ideas are getting shut down without them ever having a chance. How many great ideas never surfaced? How different would our world today be if creative ideas were openly accepted?

Your exercise is not to give in. The next time you have an idea, run it up the flagpole. If, it gets shot down, and it probably will, don't get down and discouraged. Instead, fight for your idea. Be heard. Push them on your idea. This is typically not a comfortable thing to do. What is the worst thing they can do to you, put you in front of a firing squad? **STAND UP FOR YOUR IDEA.**

"Courage is being scared to death... and saddle up anyway."
John Wayne

Find the juice

Denise Shekerjian, author of <u>Uncommon Genius</u>, wrote "Staying loose, allowing yourself the freedom to ramble, opening yourself up to outside influences, keeping a flexible mind willing to entertain all sorts of notions and avenues – this is the attitude that is most appropriate for the start of any project where the aim is to generate something new." There are many books and articles written on how to create an idea. Many of them give you a list of things you need to do to generate an idea. It is my opinion that it is very difficult to force ideas. A good creative mind generates lots of ideas. Ideas come from different places. The more open your mind is the more freely ideas will pour out. If you have checklists and a structure to generating ideas, your mind will be focusing on the checklists and not on the freedom of thinking freely and unconstrained. The bottom line is that you need to free your mind of organized thinking to let the creativity out.

Your exercise is to do creative projects that you rarely or have never done in the past. Get paper and crayons and draw anything. Don't learn how to draw, just draw. Write some poetry. Hum a new song. Free you mind. Stir up your creative juices. If you do that you will be amazed how ideas will start flowing. **START STIRRING THE JUICES.**

"To live a creative life we most first
lose the fear of being wrong."
Joseph Chilton Pearce, author

What's your first thought?

People often say, "Your first thought (or idea) is your best thought." That can be true, but it also could be a very common idea. There is a word called "ideamation." "Ideamation" is defined as the first idea that everyone thinks of. If solving your problem is obvious to others, there is a good chance they will have similar solutions. If you are trying to differentiate yourself, "ideamation" can be a bad thing. If you think you have and great idea, ask yourself, "is the idea obvious to others?" If the answer is yes, come up with another idea.

Your exercise is to take a problem that you are trying to solve to a few of you colleagues and ask them what their solution would be to the problem. If any of them have the same solution as you, go back to the drawing board and find a new solution to the problem. Your first idea may not be your best idea. **DIG DEEP AND FIND MULTIPLE IDEAS.**

"The only constant in our business is that everything is changing. We have to take advantage of change and not let it take advantage of us. We have to be ahead of the game."
Michael Dell

Sell it!

Advertising executive, David M. Ogilvy, once said, "In the modern world of business, it is useless to be a creative thinker unless you can sell what you create. Management cannot be expected to recognize a good idea unless it is presented to them by a good salesman." How true this is. I have been in the financial service business for many, many years. When I first started on Wall Street in NYC my mentor told me, "The best Research Analyst is the one who is the best salesman." Many years later that theory still holds true. A good idea isn't anything unless it is sold well.

Your exercise is to take one of the many ideas that you have written down in this book and sell it. Work on your presentation. If this is something that you are not comfortable doing, find a friend or a colleague that you think is a good sales person. Ask for their help to build yourself a sales pitch. Work on your pitch, then get a group of your friends, peers, or management team and sell them on your idea. **BECOME A SALESPERSON.**

"Every act of creation is first an act of destruction."
Pablo Picasso

Go back to school

I wrote in the first chapter of this book about how traditional schooling has thwarted CREATIVITY. Remember when we were in school drawing and our teachers were critical that we were drawing outside the lines? Now, I chuckle every time I hear someone criticize how people can't think outside-outside-box.

Your exercise is to take a half day off from what you are doing and go back to kindergarten. Yes…go back to kindergarten. Offer to help out for a couple of hours. Think of a problem you are trying to solve. While thinking of a solution to the problem and sitting among the kids, who naturally think outside-the-box, you will probably start to think differently. Believe it or not (think positively) those kindergarteners' views will rub off on you and hopefully you will have a new solution to your problem. **GO BACK TO THE FUTURE.**

"A question that sometimes drives me
hazy: am I or the others crazy?"
Albert Einstein

What is in that saying?

We often use metaphors and proverbs to describe things. How many times have you ever heard that "the grass is greener on the other side" which means things are better at some other place? How about "curiosity killed the cat?" That poor cat is dead because it was curious? I can't believe some animal loving group has not tried to eradicate that saying from our society. Think if you were to change the proverb or metaphor. Things would be different if "curiosity fed the cat," or "the grass is greener on the other side." Just by changing or taking out one word, in each proverb completely changed the meaning of that proverb.

Your exercise is to think about a metaphor or proverb that you use in your business today and change it around to change its meaning. Then think about how that new metaphor or proverb can be used to help your business. **CHANGE THE DIRECTION OF THAT SAYING AND TURN YOUR BUSINESS AROUND.**

"Every fool can see what is wrong. See what is good in it!"
Winston Churchill

Positive thinking

Composer John Cage once said, "I can't understand why people are frightened of new ideas. I'm frightened of the old ones."

Your exercise over the next week is to list every new idea you hear. Don't dismiss any. Write down three reasons why each idea is a good idea. Don't write down any reasons why it is not a good idea. This will open your mind to positive thinking. Positive thinking results in positive things. **NEGATIVE THINKING RESULTS IN NEGATIVE THINGS.**

"To improve is to change; to be perfect is to change often."
Winston Churchill

Retake that test

Albert Einstein was once asked by his students, "This is the same test as you gave us before." Einstein replied, "The same questions, but the answers are different."

Your exercise is to rewrite your business plan and chart a different course. If you don't have a fresh business plan then write two plans taking different paths. There is more than one path. **WHAT IS THE BEST PATH?**

"Children enter school as question
marks and leave as periods."
Neil Postman, author

Through a kid's eyes

So often we get comfortable with what we know. We forget what we didn't know. When we first start a new job we look around at our new surrounding with all sorts of questions and ideas. After a period of time, we fall in line with the party line. Think about how curious a child is. The opportunities are unlimited for them. They are often looking at things for the first time. They see things differently. That is how we felt when we were curious kids. It would be great to look at things in our business with no preconceived notions of how things are expected to be. It would be great to look at our business through a kid's eyes.

Your exercise is to look at your business through fresh eyes. Ask a friend, or a college student to visit your business. Explain to them what you are trying to accomplish, but don't tell them how you do it. Ask them how they would do it? They will give you that fresh view of your business. **SEE YOUR BUSINESS THROUGH A KID'S EYES.**

"Creativity can solve almost any problem. The creative act, the defeat of habit by originality, overcomes everything."
George Lois, creativity author

Where do I find ideas?

Where do you think the best? You will often read or hear from creative thinkers that the four B's are where many people do their best thinking. What are the four B's? They are:

Bars
Bathrooms
Buses
Beds

The other obvious ones that don't start with B are running, working out, waiting for the kids, carpooling, fishing, watching TV, work, etc. We all have places where we are more creative.

Your exercise is to identify where you come up with your best ideas. Once you have your places of creativity, spend more time there. I'm not saying to spend the entire work day in the shower, but I would suggest longer showers. I'm not suggesting you spend the work day running, but I would suggest running more or longer. **LET'S HIT THE SHOWER.**

People who have stopped thinking do what they have always done. DON'T STOP THINKING!

What is in the future?

I often say, "The greatest accomplishments in history have yet to be achieved." There will always be a greater play, song, painting, etc. Records will be broken. Things will be invented. The world as we know it is always evolving. Think about your life. How has it evolved since your birth? How will it evolve going forward?

Your exercise is to think about your business today. What will it look like 1, 3, 5, 10, 50 and 100 hundred years from now? Don't worry about being wrong. Who will be around in 100 years to tell you that you were wrong? Set out with what you know today and dream about what the future could look like. **DREAM BIG OR GO HOME.**

"The most powerful factors in the world are clear
ideas in the minds of energetic men of good will."
J. Arthur Thomson, author

The century of ideas

Seth Godin, who is a marketing expert and author, once said "the first 100 years of our country's history were about who could build the biggest, most efficient farm. And the second century focused on the race to build factories. Welcome to the third century, folks. The third century is about ideas."

Your exercise is to go to Seth Godin's blog and sign up. This blog is full of ideas and motivation. He gets your CREATIVITY juices flowing. **SQUEEZE THOSE JUICES OUT.**

"The social consequences of releasing creative
abilities are potentially enormous."
J.P. Guilford, researcher of creativity

List your office

Have you ever noticed how positive all real estate listings are? If the rooms are small, they call them charming. If there is a large room, it is spacious. A nice patio is an outdoor living area. They accent the positive and they deemphasize the faults.

Your exercise is to build a real estate listing for your work area. If you have an office, describe your office and neighboring offices. If you are in a cubicle, accent the positives of the space and deemphasize the negatives. **SELL YOUR CUBICLE!**

CHAPTER 3

Let's CREATE

CREATE

CREATE

CREATE

CREATE

CREATE

CREATE

CREATE

CREATE

CREATE

CREATE

CREATE

CREATE

CREATE

CREATE

CREATE

CREATE

CREATE

CREATE

CREATE

CREATE

CREATE

CREATE

CREATE

CREATE

CREATE

CREATE

CREATE

CREATE

CREATE

CREATE

CREATE

CREATE

CREATE

CREATE

CREATE

CREATE

Conclusion

Thank you for reading the book. I hope I was able to get you to think about getting creative in the business world. Creativity has always come easy to me, but exercising it has kept it alive and sharp. The gift, that we all have, needs to be nurtured and cherished.

I hope that you took the opportunity to write down your ideas. Please go back through the book and read your notes. The next great idea could be there. Most of all, I hope I have inspired you to have the COURAGE to CREATE.

mbalch@thebalchgroup.com

Printed in the United States
By Bookmasters